The Butterfly Book

A Kid's Guide to Attracting, Raising, and Keeping Butterflies

by Kersten Hamilton

John Muir Publications
Santa Fe, New Mexico

W9-BWJ-752

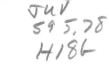

Dedicated to the original and honorary PDs: Jennie, Tammy, Shawna, Nadia, James, Meghan, and Mark Isaac from Kersten (Beauty products? I don't need no beauty products!) Hamilton

Special thanks to Thomas C. Emmel, Professor and Director, Division of Lepidoptera Research, University of Florida, and Professor Orley R. Taylor, Department of Entomology, University of Kansas.

John Muir Publications, P.O. Box 613, Santa Fe, NM 87504
Text copyright © 1997 by Kersten Hamilton
Cover, illustrations, and maps © 1997 by John Muir Publications

Printed in the United States of America by Burton & Mayer Inc.
First edition. First printing March 1997.

Library of Congress Cataloging-in-Publication Data
Hamilton, Kersten R.
    The butterfly book : attracting, raising, and keeping butterflies / by Kersten Hamilton.
        p.   cm.
Includes index.
Summary: Explains how to attract, identify, and raise butterflies.
ISBN 1-56261-309-X
1. Butterflies—Juvenile literature. 2. Butterfly attracting—Juvenile literature. 3. Butterflies as pets—Juvenile literature.
[1. Butterflies as pets.] I. Title.
QL544.2.H35   1997
595.78'9—dc20   96-33172
                                                                                        CIP
                                                                                        AC

Design Janine Lehmann
Illustrations Melissa Tandysh
Butterfly Guide illustrations and maps Susan Harrison

Distributed to the book trade by
Publishers Group West
Emeryville, California

Photo Credits
Page 3—San Diego Zoo; Pages 4, 13, 14 (left), 19, 33, 35 (both)—Don Jarrett; Pages 5 (left, right), 6 (left, right), 12 (both), 14 (center), 15, 16, 17, 18, 20, 23, 25, 29, 34—Bob Wilson; Page 5 (center)—David M. Wright; Page 6 (center), 7—Thomas J. Allen; Pages 14 (right), 21, 24, 27, 28, 30—Paul A. Opler; Page 29 (left, center)—Steven Cary; Page 31—Evi Buckner; Page 36—Terry G. Murphy/Butterfly Pavilion and Insect Center; Page 37 (all images)—Dr. Jacqueline Y. Miller; Back cover—David M. Wright

You're lying in the grass on a perfect spring day. Suddenly, a shadow sweeps past. Look! Up in the sky! It's a bird . . . it's a plane . . . it's a butterfly!

A butterfly is one of the most amazing creatures on Earth. Its delicate antennae can sense wind speed and direction and "smell" flowers. Chemical sensors in its feet allow it to "taste" the leaves and flowers it walks on. Its eyes detect light waves that humans can't see, allowing it to see more colors than any other creature on earth. These insects live everywhere people live, even in the heart of the city. You can hunt them in wild and weedy places, invite them into your yard, or even raise them in your bedroom.

With this book you'll learn how to attract and care for butterflies.

Getting to Know the Butterfly

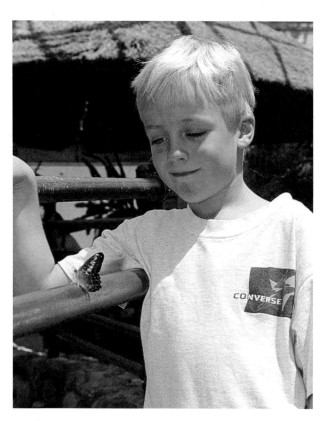

Understanding a butterfly's **life cycle**, or the changes it goes through, will help you find butterflies to watch and to raise. It's much easier to collect butterfly eggs or caterpillars than it is to catch a winged adult. Learning about their life cycle will also help you take care of your butterflies once you've caught them.

The first stage in a butterfly's life is as an **ovum**, or egg. The caterpillar, or **larva**, that hatches from the tiny egg doesn't look like our idea of a butterfly at all. It looks like a worm! It must go through **complete metamorphosis**, or total change, before it becomes a winged adult.

A caterpillar is an insect. All insects have three body parts: the **head**, **thorax**, and **abdomen**. The caterpillar's head is encased in a hard shell called a **head capsule**. Under the head are powerful **mandibles**, or jaws. Beneath the mandibles are **spinnerets** that produce silk threads. Caterpillars may use silk to make shelters or to drop from one leaf to another like a mountain climber on a rope.

Caterpillars grow in stages called **instars**. The first instar begins when the caterpillar crawls out of its egg. Its tough skin, or **exoskeleton**, doesn't grow, but its body underneath the exoskeleton does. When the exoskeleton becomes too tight, the caterpillar stops eating for about a day. Then the head capsule pops off and a new head capsule that has been growing behind it emerges. The exoskeleton splits down the back, and the caterpillar crawls out. It has a new, larger exoskeleton. The second instar has begun. The caterpillar will go through four to seven instars.

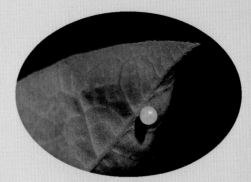

Caterpillar egg

The first instar

A caterpillar and its exoskeleton

5

Monarch chrysalis

Inside the chrysalis,
a caterpillar changes
into an adult butterfly

The crumpled, wet
wings of a newly
emerged butterfly

When the caterpillar is finished growing, it **pupates**. This means it changes from a caterpillar into a **pupa**, which is also called a **chrysalis**. The caterpillar crawls up on a twig or wall and spins a silk pad. It fastens itself securely to the pad with little hooks and hangs upside down. Once more, the old exoskeleton splits. This time a chrysalis emerges. Sealed inside its mummy-like pupa, the caterpillar's flesh and organs dissolve. It turns into a living soup! The few groups of cells that remain together carry the blueprint for an adult butterfly. The caterpillar soup re-forms around these cell groups into the wings, legs, and body of an adult.

A New Butterfly Greets the World

When the adult butterfly emerges from the chrysalis, its tube-like mouth, called a **proboscis**, is in two straight pieces. Its wings are crumpled and wet. The butterfly pumps fluid from its body through hollow veins in its wings. Its wings grow longer, fan out, and become stiff. As its wings dry, the butterfly fits the two sides of its proboscis together to form a straw and rolls it neatly under its head. Within a few hours of emerging, the butterfly is ready to fly in search of food and a mate.

• The butterfly's **compound eyes** (eyes made of many separate lenses) are large, jewel-like globes. The multiple lenses allow the butterfly to see in all directions at once. The clearness of the image the butterfly sees depends on how many lenses are aimed at an object. The farther away an object is, the fewer lenses will be aimed at it. This makes the butterfly extremely nearsighted.

• Between its compound eyes, the butterfly has two long, delicate **antennae**. These are actually the butterfly's nose! Chemical receptors in the antennae can detect tiny particles, giving the butterfly a keen sense of smell. The antennae's pressure receptors detect changes in wind speed.

• Under the eyes on each side of the butterfly's proboscis are hairy structures called **palpi**. Some scientists think palpi protect the proboscis. Whatever their purpose is, palpi look a lot like a mustache!

• The **tarsi**, the butterfly's feet, have tiny claws on the tips for gripping petals and leaves. The rear tarsi have chemical sensors that let the butterfly "taste" the plants it walks on.

• **Wing veins** and tiny colored **scales** make the patterns on the butterfly's two **forewings** and two **hindwings.**

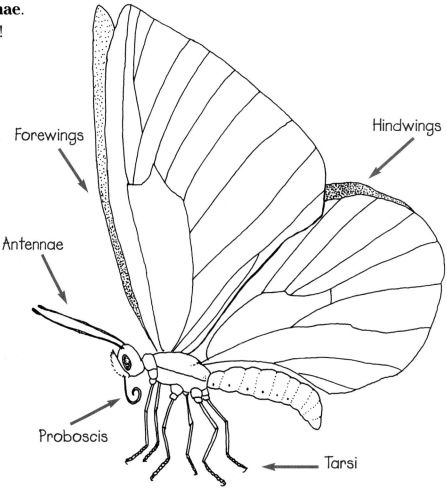

Forewings

Hindwings

Antennae

Proboscis

Tarsi

When Butterflies Ruled the Earth

Butterflies have been around for a very long time. When *Tyrannosaurus rex* roamed the Earth, the land where you live was filled with butterflies. The woodlands, deserts, and swamps provided everything a butterfly needed:

Wildflowers

Butterflies drink a sweet liquid called **nectar** that is found in many flowers. Scientists think that petals of wildflowers, which reflect **ultraviolet light**, flash like neon signs to a butterfly's specialized eyes.

Larval food plants

Tasting with your toes might seem funny, but it can be very important to butterflies. A butterfly flitting from leaf to leaf may be "tasting" each one with her tarsi, searching for the right caterpillar food plant on which to lay her eggs.

Banks for basking

Butterflies are cold-blooded, which means their bodies can't make heat the way bodies of warm-blooded creatures can. A butterfly sits in the sun to warm its muscles so it can fly. This is called **basking**.

Puddles

Butterflies can't drink from deep or fast-flowing water. They prefer sipping from shallow puddles.

Shelter

A butterfly chrysalis can't crawl or fly. Its only defense against predators is **camouflage**, which means blending in with its surroundings. Chrysalises may look like dead leaves or stems.

Attracting Butterflies

No one knows why the dinosaurs died out while the butterflies lived on. But today, descendants of the butterflies that flew among the dinosaurs are living all around you. You can invite them to visit by turning your yard, patio, or a windowsill into a **butterfly garden**.

A shallow dish or old bird bath filled with flat stones makes a good butterfly puddle. Rocks, grassy banks, or windowsills are perfect spots for basking. Providing a proper menu takes a little more work.

BUTTERFLY GUIDE

The Butterfly Guide, which begins on the following page will help you identify the butterflies and caterpillars you find. Under each butterfly, you'll find a picture of its caterpillar and larval food plant, which is the plant the caterpillar eats. The colored zones on the map will show you where the butterfly can be found.

- Zone 1—Ore., Wash., southern British Columbia
- Zone 2—Ariz., Calif., Nev.
- Zone 3—Colo., Idaho, Mont., Utah, Wyo., southern Alberta, southern Saskatchewan, southwest Manitoba
- Zone 4—N.Mex., Tex.
- Zone 5—Ill., Iowa, Kans., Minn., Mo., Nebr., N.Dak., Okla., S.Dak., Wis., southeast Manitoba
- Zone 6—Ala., Ark., Fla., Ga., Ky., La., Miss., N.C., S.C., Tenn., Va.
- Zone 7—Conn., Del., Ind., Maine, Md., Mass., Mich., N.H., N.J., N.Y., Ohio, Pa., R.I., Vt., D.C., W.Va., southern Ontario, southern Quebec

BUTTERFLY GUIDE

MONARCH
(Danaus plexippus)

Larval food plant:
milkweed

Found in zones:

A Butterfly's Banquet

Wildflowers are a great nectar source for butterflies, and they may already be growing in your yard. A butterfly will drink nectar from garden flowers, too, but many flowers that look beautiful to us just don't appeal to butterflies. A butterfly might starve to death in a rose garden because roses have very little nectar. How can you tell which flowers have lots of nectar? Watch for bees. Bees and butterflies are attracted to many of the same flowers.

Gardening Tips

Butterflies are attracted to flowers by their color and their scent. Planting flowers in groups of one color makes them easier to find. Many butterflies are attracted to white, purple, and yellow flowers. It's also good to plant flowers of different sizes. Tall flowers with wide petals, like cosmos, make good landing pads for big butterflies. Tiny butterflies can feed at low-lying plants that big butterflies may not be able to reach.

🦋 Fast Food for Butterflies

Whether your garden is large or small, you can make a fast-food restaurant that is ideal for butterflies. Cut purple and yellow sponges into flower shapes. Place them in the shallow dish. Mix one-third of a cup of sugar into one cup of water. Stir until the sugar dissolves. Pour it in the dish with the sponges. Fill the dish almost to the top of the sponge flowers. The tops of your fake flowers should be wet to the touch. Butterflies will land on them and sip the sugar water.

Cut watermelon or some other ripe fruit into pieces. Put the fruit on a plate beside your dish of flowers. Set the food in a sunny place for butterflies to find.

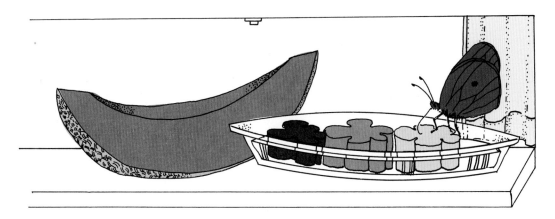

AMERICAN PAINTED LADY
(Vanessa virginiensis)

Larval food plant:
everlasting

Found in zones:

Creating a Caterpillar Café

Adult butterflies can sip nectar from the flowers of many different plants, but caterpillars have a harder time finding food. Some, like the zebra longwing caterpillar, can eat the leaves of only one type of plant.

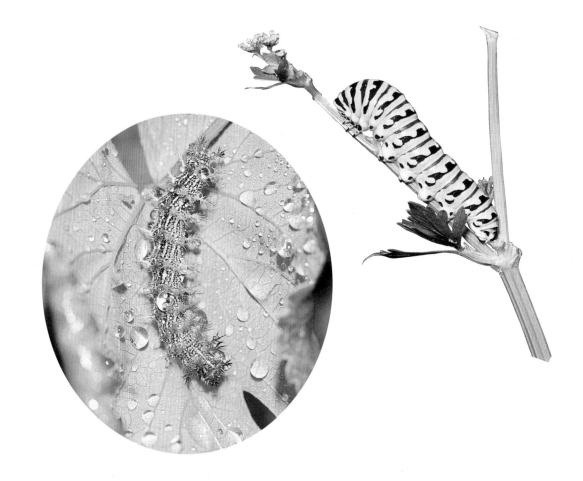

Most butterflies lay their eggs on the food plants that are eaten by their caterpillars. For example, a monarch butterfly lays her eggs on the milkweed plant because her newly-hatched caterpillars eat the leaves of the milkweed. If this plant is unavailable, the female butterfly won't have anywhere to lay her eggs. That's why it's important to grow caterpillar food plants along with your flowers.

Warning!

Caterpillars have many enemies. Birds and beetles gobble up butterfly eggs and caterpillars. Parasitoid wasps, which lay their eggs inside butterfly eggs or caterpillars' bodies, destroy many more. A female butterfly may lay hundreds of eggs in your garden, but only a few will live to become adult butterflies.

BUTTERFLY GUIDE

PIPEVINE SWALLOWTAIL
(*Battus philenor*)

Larval food plant:
pipevine

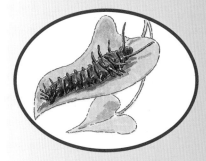

Found in zones:

15

GREAT SPANGLED FRITILLARY
(Speyeria cybele)

Larval food plant:
violets

Found in zones:

Making a Caterpillar Corral

You can make a "corral" to protect your caterpillars from birds and insect predators. You will need a large piece of netting, a needle and thread, and two pieces of string. Stitch the two longest edges of the netting together to make a tube. Slide the netting tube over the branch where the caterpillars are feeding. Tie both ends of the tube with a string. When most of the leaves in the corral are gone, move the larvae and corral to another branch.

On a patio or windowsill where the caterpillar's food plant is in a flower pot, you can put netting around the whole plant. Bend two pieces of wire into U shapes. Press the ends of the wires into the potting soil at the edge of the planter. The wires should crisscross. The top of each upside-down U should be a few inches taller than your plant. Drape netting over your wires. The netting should reach about halfway down the side of your pot. Use string to secure the netting around the pot.

![butterfly icon] # A Butterfly Tent Trap

One way to get close to butterflies in your garden is to catch them in a tent trap. To make a trap, you'll need a 2' x 2' square of netting, four long pieces of strong string, a 2' x 2' square piece of cardboard, and four safety pins.

1. Poke a hole in each corner of the cardboard. Thread a string though each hole. Tie a knot on the end of the string so that it won't slip back though the hole.

2. Tie all 4 strings together about 24 inches above the board. Make a small hole in the middle of your netting. Push the ends of your strings though the hole so that the netting hangs down like a tent. Gather the extra material at the corners and pin it to the strings.

3. The top of the tent should be at the knot where your strings join. The bottom of the tent should be a few inches above your board. Hang the tent from a branch. Put some overripe fruit in the middle of your cardboard, directly under the tent. When the butterflies that are attracted to the fruit try to fly away, they'll be caught in the tent. After you've studied the butterflies, raise one side of the tent to release them.

BUTTERFLY GUIDE

EUROPEAN CABBAGE WHITE
(Pieris rapae)

Larval food plant:
cabbage

Found in zones:

BUTTERFLY GUIDE

ZEBRA LONGWING
(Heliconius charitonius)

Larval food plant:
passionflower

Found in zones:

Butterflies in Your Bedroom?

Would you like to share your bedroom with a butterfly? When you raise a butterfly, you can observe every stage of its life, from the time the tiny larva crawls out of its egg to the moment the butterfly spreads its wings. Before you move a butterfly into your house, you must prepare a safe place to keep it and learn how to take care of it as it grows.

Getting Ready

Caterpillars can live anywhere in your house. You can raise them in paper cups, jars, or boxes with holes in the lid. Any container that keeps the larvae dry while allowing air to circulate is fine. The biggest threats to the health of your caterpillars are bacteria and mold. Caterpillars don't need much air to breathe, but fresh air helps keep bacteria and mold from growing.

Your caterpillar cage should have a rough surface such as cardboard, window screen, or a tiny branch near the top. The rough surface will allow the caterpillar to attach the silk pad for the chrysalis. As soon as the caterpillar pupates, you should move the chrysalis to a cage large enough for the adult to spread its wings when it emerges.

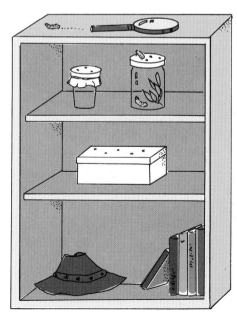

Handling Caterpillars

Always be gentle when you handle caterpillars. Large caterpillars can be moved with your fingers. (Don't pick up fuzzy caterpillars. They might give you a rash.) Tiny caterpillars can be carried on a leaf or moved with a small paintbrush.

QUEEN
(Danaus gilippus)

Larval food plant:
milkweed

Found in zones:

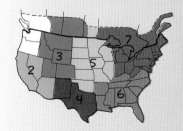

19

BUTTERFLY GUIDE

QUESTION MARK
(*Polygonia interrogationis*)

Larval food plant:
hops

Found in zones:

Caterpillar Cuisine

Caterpillars get all the water they need from the green plants they eat. If the plants are dry or wilted, your caterpillar won't get enough moisture. To keep the plant cuttings fresh in the cage, wrap the stems in wet paper towels, then put the wrapped stems in a plastic bag. Twist a rubber band around the top of the bag to keep the moisture in and the caterpillars out. Never put water in your cage—caterpillars can't swim! Part of the plant matter that goes into a caterpillar comes out its other end as waste. Caterpillar droppings are called frass, and they are usually brown or dark green. Frass should be cleaned from the cage every day.

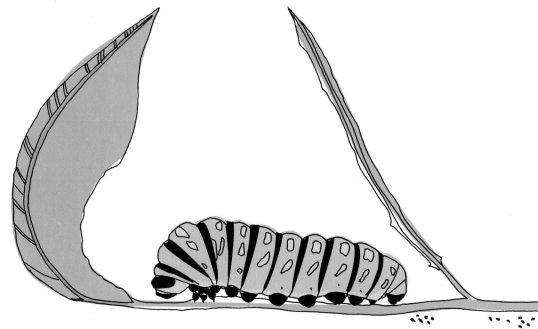

A shoe box makes a great caterpillar or butterfly cage. You can raise up to five butterflies in it at one time! Set the shoe box on end, cover the front of the box with nylon netting, and tie it with a string.

BUTTERFLY GUIDE

WEST COAST LADY
(Vanessa annabella)

Larval food plant:
hollyhock

Found in zones:

After Your Butterfly Emerges

If you would like to keep a butterfly for a few days after it emerges from its chrysalis, mix up some butterfly food using the recipe from page 13. Add a pinch of bee pollen (you can buy this at your local health food store) to the mixture. The pollen provides your butterfly with **amino acids**—the building blocks of protein—and helps it live longer. Pour the mixture over a sponge in a shallow dish in the bottom of your butterfly cage.

If your butterfly hasn't eaten yet a day after it has emerged, hold it with one hand and gently uncurl its proboscis with a toothpick. Dip the tip of the proboscis in the sugar water. If the butterfly doesn't start sipping, it's not hungry. Its proboscis will curl up by itself. After two or three days, release the butterfly so it can find a mate.

The Hunt

Making a Hunter's Kit

Your cages are ready. You know how to care for caterpillars and butterflies. It's time to prepare a butterfly hunter's kit! Here's what should be in it:

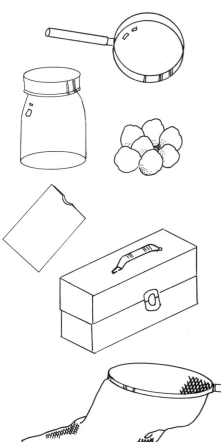

- **Magnifying glass**—to examine your specimens

- **Baby food jars or film canisters**—to carry caterpillars, chrysalises, and butterfly eggs

- **Cotton balls**—for padding

- **Glassine envelopes**—to hold your butterflies when you take them home. Glassine envelopes are clear envelopes used by stamp collectors to store their stamps.

- **Plastic or metal box**—to hold your butterfly envelopes

- **Butterfly net**—for catching the butterflies!

GREAT PURPLE HAIRSTREAK
(Atlides halesus)

Larval food plant: mistletoe

Found in zones:

BUTTERFLY GUIDE

ORANGE SULPHUR
(Colias eurytheme)

Larval food plant:
alfalfa clover

Found in zones:

24

Making a Butterfly Net

To complete your buterfly hunter's kit, you'll need a butterfly net at least 2 feet deep. Buy one at a science store, or make your own with a broomstick, coat hanger, netting, and duct tape. Here's how to do it:

1. Straighten out the hook on the coat hanger. Bend the rest of the coat hanger into a circle. Measure the size of your circle with a cloth measuring tape.

2. Cut a long rectangle of netting. The short side of your rectangle should be just a little larger than the measurement of your hanger circle. The other side should be about 2 feet long. Fold the netting in half lengthwise. Sew the side and bottom to make a bag.

3. Fold the top of your bag over the wire circle (about half an inch) and sew it. Tape the straightened hook to the end of the broomstick with duct tape.

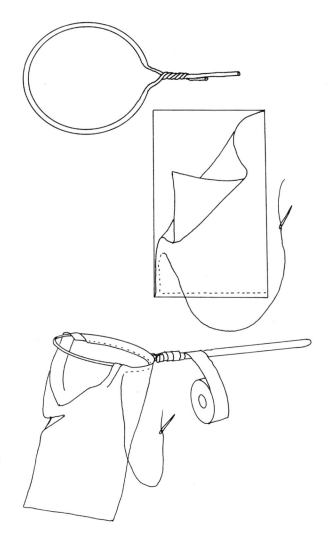

How to Find Butterfly Eggs, Caterpillars, and Chrysalises

Vegetable gardens, flower beds, and empty lots full of grasses and wildflowers are good places to hunt. If you notice that a butterfly is attracted to certain leaves instead of flowers, check the plant carefully for caterpillars or eggs. Watch for butterflies landing on small plants, bushes, and even trees. For example, great spangled fritillary caterpillars eat the leaves of violets. Mourning cloak caterpillars munch on the leaves of willow, aspen, or cottonwood trees.

What You'll Need:

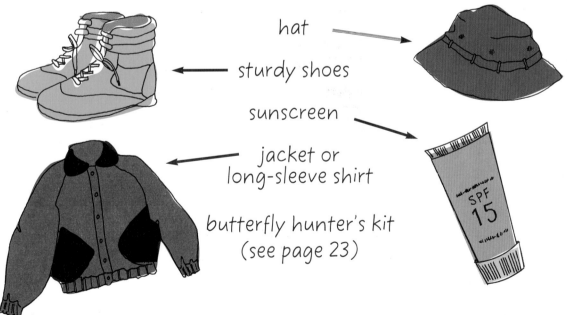

hat

sturdy shoes

sunscreen

jacket or long-sleeve shirt

butterfly hunter's kit (see page 23)

SPF 15

BUTTERFLY GUIDE

ANISE SWALLOWTAIL
(Papilio zelicaon)

Larval food plant:
fennel, dill, carrot, parsley

Found in zones:

1
3
5
2
4

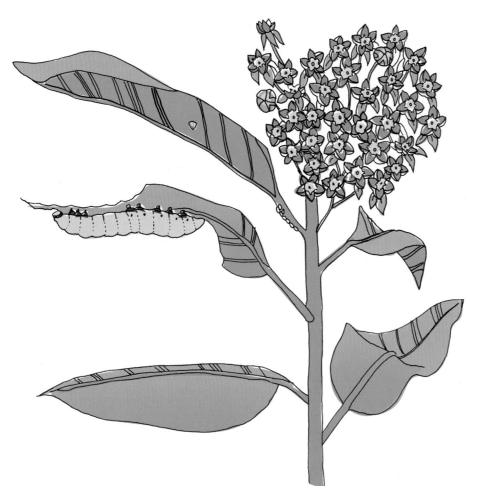

Butterfly Eggs

Many butterflies lay their eggs on the bottom of a leaf or on the stem of the plant. Some lay a single egg, but others lay clusters of eggs.

When you find butterfly eggs, remove the entire stem and leaves of the plant on which the eggs are attached. Keep the leaves fresh by wrapping the stems in damp paper towels. To keep from damaging the eggs, place the leaves and the damp towels in a film canister or baby food jar lined with cotton.

Caterpillars

The best way to find caterpillars is to look for leaves that show signs of having been chewed. Caterpillars may be feeding on the underside of the leaf, especially during the heat of the day. Remove the whole leaf the caterpillar is feeding on. This way, it will be able to eat on the way to its new home. These are the kind of leaves your caterpillar will need to eat until it pupates.

Chrysalises

Chewed leaves can be a clue to finding chrysalises, too. The caterpillar will crawl up on a wall, tree, or bush near its food plant to pupate. Gently take the whole stem or piece of bark the chrysalis is attached to and put it in your padded container.

When you place the chrysalis in your cage, tie a string around the bark or twig the chrysalis is attached to. Tie the other end of the string around a twig or stick near the top of your cage. Be sure there is enough room in the cage for the butterfly to spread its wings when it emerges.

GRAY HAIRSTREAK
(Strymon melinus)

Larval food plant:
mallow

Found in zones:

PURPLISH COPPER
(Lycaena helloides)

Larval food plant:
dock

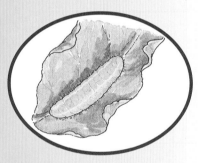

Found in zones:

Creating a Caterpillar Café

Catching a butterfly with a net takes practice. If you're careful to follow these steps, though, you might net a butterfly on your first hunting trip:

• Wait until the butterfly is sitting on a leaf or flower. Flip the net over the butterfly, then quickly turn the handle. This will close the mouth of the net.

• Grasp the butterfly right through the net. Make sure its wings are folded over its back. Hold it gently by the front of its wings with the thumb and forefinger of one hand.

• Reach into the net with your other hand and clasp the butterfly firmly by the base of all four wings. Now carefully fold the net away from your butterfly.

• With its wings still folded, carefully slip the butterfly into an envelope. Put the envelope in a metal or plastic box to keep it from being crushed.

Congratulations on your first catch!

Reading a Butterfly's Life Story

If you're a careful observer, you can learn alot about the butterflies you catch. For example:

• A butterfly whose wings show no rips, tears, or missing scales has emerged from its chrysalis very recently.

• A clean, V-shaped snip out of a wing is a sign that the butterfly has survived a bird attack. The V shape is the mark left by a bird's beak.

• A butterfly with faded, ragged wings is probably nearing the end of its life. If it's a member of a migratory species, it may have flown thousands of miles to reach your yard.

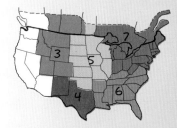
29

BUTTERFLY GUIDE

MYLITTA CRESCENT
(Phyciodes mylitta)

Larval food plant:
thistle

Found in zones:

Becoming a Butterfly Doctor

The veins in a butterfly's wings work like the sticks in a kite. They keep the butterfly's wings stiff. If the vein on the front edge of a butterfly's wing breaks, the wing is uselss. The butterfly will die because it can't fly in search of food. You can mend a butterfly's broken wing with half-inch round paper stickers called merchandise markers. You can buy these at office-supply stores. Hold the butterfly with one hand and gently rub off the scales around the break with the thumb and forefinger of your other hand. Be sure to rub them off on both sides of the wing, top and bottom.

Stick half of the sticker on the front of the butterfly's wing, just over the break. Fold it around the broken vein so that the other half sticks to the back of the wing. Press firmly. Some butterflies have been found 1,000 miles from where their wings were mended.

Keep Your Butterfly Safe

Remember, all living creatures should be handled with care and respect. Butterflies should never be carried in jars. They might flap and damage their wings. You should put the butterfly in a small glassine envelope with its wings folded above its back. Put the envelope in a plastic or metal box so the butterfly won't get crushed.

Keep all your live specimens cool. If you leave them in the sun, the heat can kill them. Always put them in a safe cage as soon as you get home.

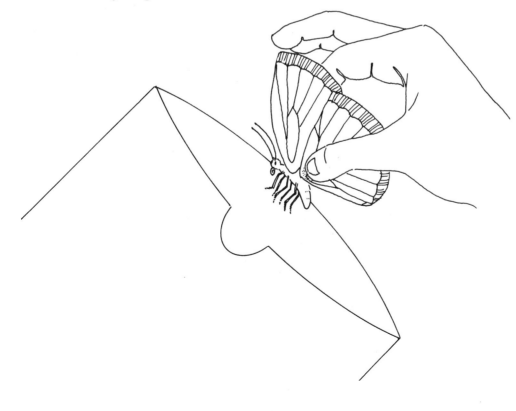

FIELD CRESCENT
(Phyciodes campestris)

Larval food plant:
aster

Found in zones:

31

Butterfly Facts

Butterflies in Winter

Even though you may not see them, there are butterflies in your neighborhood—even in the coldest winter months. In winter, butterflies are in **diapause,** a type of hibernation. In ovum, larva, or pupa form, they may be sleeping in a sheltered quiet place. A few species even live through the winter as adults, hanging inside hollow logs, in woodpiles, or under the eaves of your house.

Butterflies in diapause don't need food, but they need shelter. You can create a hibernation shelter by cutting an entrance in the plastic lid of a coffee can. Put some leaves and twigs inside the can for insulation.

Bizarre Butterfly Behavior

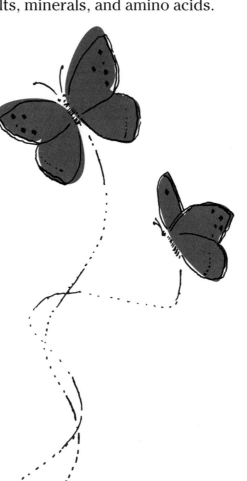

Sometimes you'll find groups of butterflies on patches of damp sand or mud. You may find a butterfly sipping liquid from animal droppings or an animal carcass. Why? Nectar is sweet, but it's not a balanced diet for a butterfly. Butterflies also need salts, minerals, and amino acids. Moist sand contains salts and minerals. Animal waste and carcasses contain salts, minerals, and amino acids.

Sky Dancing

Many butterflies species look alike, even to other butterflies. Butterflies have developed special clues to help them find a mate of their own species. The first clue is the color and pattern on their wings. The second is a scent butterflies give off. The third clue is a mating dance. If a butterfly of the opposite sex is the right color, smells right, and knows all the steps to the dance, he or she is the right mate.

BUTTERFLY GUIDE

BLACK SWALLOWTAIL
(Papilio polyxenes)

Larval food plant:
dill, carrot, Queen Ann's Lace

Found in zones:

BUTTERFLY GUIDE

VARIEGATED FRITILLARY
(Euptoieta claudia)

Larval food plant:
violets and pansies

Found in zones:

Perching and Patrolling

Some male butterflies are territorial. They pick a territory or a specific area, either perching somewhere to watch over it, or gliding through it on patrol. Whenever they see something that might be a female, they fly to investigate. If it's another male, they may have a fierce butterfly fight, spinning and batting each other until one gives up and goes away. Male butterflies have even been known to attack birds.

Save the Earth by Raising Butterflies

Planting flowers to attract butterflies, watching them in your garden, and raising them in your bedroom is more than just fun. It's also helpful to the environment. People have studied butterflies for thousands of years, but we're just now beginning to understand their importance to human beings.

All living creatures on our planet, including human beings, depend on plants for food. Most plants depend on insects to fertilize their seeds by carrying pollen from flower to flower. Butterflies gather pollen on their bodies as they sip nectar, carrying it with them from plant to plant. Butterflies and moths pollinate more plants than any other insect except the bee.

BUTTERFLY GUIDE

SPICEBUSH SWALLOWTAIL
(Papilio troilus)

Larval food plant:
sassafras

Found in zones:

35

Some Butterflies That Need Your Help

As cities and farmlands expand, fields of wildflowers and marshy wetlands—home to many butterflies—grow smaller or disappear altogether. Some places where butterflies could live, such as yards and roadsides, are sprayed with **insecticides**, chemicals that kill insect pests. Unfortunately, insecticides kill butterflies, too. Fifteen varieties of North American butterflies are on the list of threatened and endangered species. You can find pictures of some endangered butterflies on page 37. The map will show you where they live.

There are several things you can do to help butterflies:
- Don't catch or collect endangered butterflies.
- Never use insecticides in your garden.
- Join an organization that is working to save butterflies. You'll find a list of these organizations on page 38.

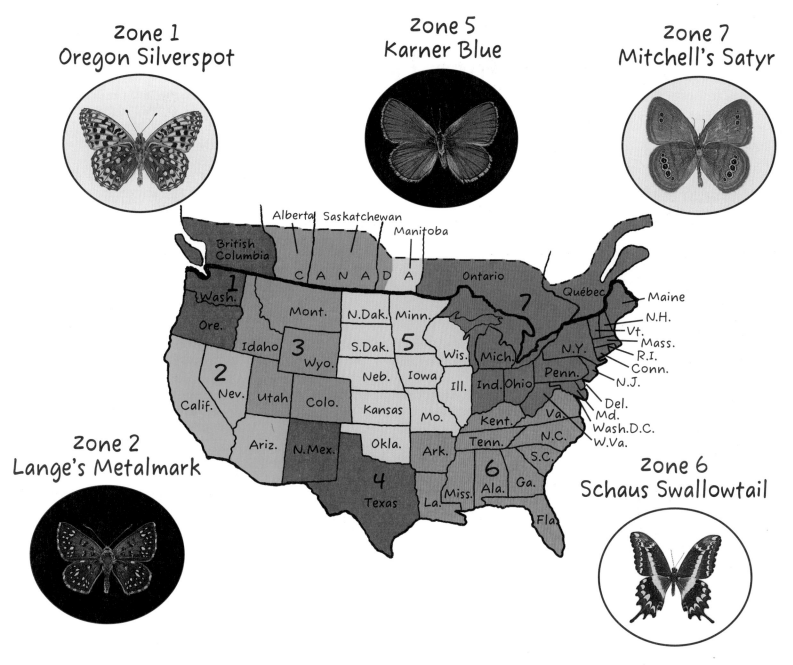

Zone 1
Oregon Silverspot

Zone 5
Karner Blue

Zone 7
Mitchell's Satyr

Zone 2
Lange's Metalmark

Zone 6
Schaus Swallowtail

Alberta Saskatchewan

Manitoba

British
Columbia

C A N A D A

Ontario

Québec

Maine

1

Wash.

N.H.
Vt.
Mass.
R.I.
Conn.
N.J.

Ore.

Mont.

N.Dak.

Minn.

Idaho

3

S.Dak.

5

Wis.

Mich.

N.Y.

Wyo.

Neb.

Iowa

Ill.

Ind. Ohio

Penn.

2

Nev.

Utah

Colo.

Del.
Md.
Wash.D.C.
W.Va.

Calif.

Kansas

Mo.

Kent.

Va.

Ariz.

N.Mex.

Okla.

Ark.

Tenn.

N.C.

S.C.

4

6

Texas

La.

Miss.

Ala.

Ga.

Fla.

Resource Guide

Where to Order Caterpillars Through the Mail

Insect Lore Products
P.O. Box 1535
Shafter, CA 93263
(800) 548-3284
Free catalog on request

If you would like to order monarch larvae, and you live east of the Rocky Mountains, contact:

Monarch Watch
c/o Orley Taylor
Department of Entomology
University of Kansas
Lawrence, Kansas 66045-2106
(913) 864-4051

If you live west of the Rocky Mountains:

The Monarch Program
P.O. Box 178671
San Diego, CA 92117

Mail-Order Butterfly Nets and Other Neat Stuff

Acorn Naturalists
17300 East 17th Street, #J-236

Tustin, CA 92680
(714) 838-4888

American Biological Supply Company
2405 NW 66th Court
Gainesville, FL 32606
(301) 747-1797

BioQuip Products
17803 LaSalle Avenue
Gardena, CA 90248
(213) 324-0620

Organizations for People Who Love Butterflies

North American Butterfly Association
4 Delaware Road
Morristown, NJ 07960-5725

Association for Tropical Lepidoptera
P.O. Box 14210
Gainesville, FL 32614-1210

Xerces Society
10 Southwest Ash Street
Portland, OR 97204
(503) 232-6639

National Wildlife Federation
Urban Wildlife Programs
1400 16th Street NW
Washington, DC 20036-2266
(202) 797-6800

Young Entomologists' Society
International Headquarters
1915 Peggy Place
Lansing, MI 48910
(517) 887-0499

Butterflies on the World Wide Web

The Butterfly Site
http://mgfx.com/butterfly

The Smithsonian Institution's Butterfly Garden
http://photo2.si.edu/bflyhome.html

Wings and Waterfalls
http://www.npbg.org/wings/

Niagra Parks Botanical Gardens
School of Horticulture & Butterfly Conservatory
http://www.npbg.org

Glossarized Index

abdomen—the last segment of an insect's body, **5**

amino acids—the building blocks of protein, **22, 23**

antenna (plural: antennae)—a sensory organ on the head of an insect. Butterflies detect scents and wind speed with their antennae, **3, 8**

bask—what a butterfly does to raise its body temperature. Butterflies bask in the sun to warm themselves, **10, 11**

butterfly garden—a garden with nectar and larval food plants for butterflies, **11**

camouflage—colors, patterns, or shapes that make chrysalises, caterpillars, or butterflies difficult to see, **10**

caterpillar—the second stage of a butterfly's life cycle. Also called a larva, **4, 5, 6, 9, 11, 15, 16, 19, 20, 21, 23, 25, 26, 27**

chrysalis—the third stage of a butterfly's life cycle. Also called a pupa, **6, 7, 10, 19, 23, 27**

complete metamorphosis—the series of changes (ovum, larva, pupa, adult) that butterflies and moths go through during their life cycle, **4**

compound eye—an eye made of many separate eye units. Scientists believe that a butterfly's brain puts many images together into one fairly clear image. Some butterflies have as few as 50 separate lenses in each compound eye, others have hundreds, **7**

diapause—a period of "sleep" or hibernation. Different kinds of butterflies go through diapause at different stages. Diapause can occur either in winter or in a hot dry season when there is no food supply, **32**

exoskeleton—an external supportive skin. Our bodies are supported by an internal skeleton. Insects have no bones inside and their bodies are supported by their tough skin, **5, 6**

forewings—the front set of a butterfly's wings, **8**

frass—caterpillar droppings, usually dark green or brown colored, **21**

head—the first segment of an insect, **5**

head capsule—a hard shell that protects the caterpillar's head. A head capsule looks like a miniature helmet and goggles, **5**

hindwings—the rear set of a butterfly's wings, **8**

insecticide—a chemical designed to kill insects, **36**

instar—the period of growth from the time a caterpillar sheds its skin to the next time it sheds its skin, **5**

Glossarized Index

larva (plural: larvae)—the second stage of a butterfly's life cycle. Also called a caterpillar, **4, 5, 16, 18, 19, 21, 32**

larval food plant—the plant a particular caterpillar eats, **9, 11**

life cycle—the series of changes a living creature goes through during its lifetime, **4**

mandibles—jaws, **5**

nectar—sweet liquid found in flowers, **9, 11, 12, 14, 22, 33**

ovum (plural: ova)—an egg. The first stage in a butterfly's life cycle, **4**

palp (plural: palpi)—mustache-like structures on each side of a butterfly's proboscis, **8**

Parasitoid wasp—a type of wasp that lays its eggs inside a butterfly egg or under the skin of a caterpillar. An infested butterfly egg may have dozens of wasps growing inside it, **15**

proboscis—a butterfly's tube-like mouth, **7, 8, 22**

pupa (plural: pupae)—the third stage of a butterfly's life cycle. Also called a chrysalis, **6**

pupate—become a pupa, **6, 19**

scales—tiny shingle-like structures on a butterfly's wing. A butterfly's scales are modified hairs, **8**

spinneret—an organ under the larva's head that spins silk, **5**

tarsus (plural: tarsi)—the jointed end of a butterfly's leg—its "foot," **8**

thorax—the second segment of an insect body, **5**

ultraviolet light—light with wavelengths shorter than the wavelengths of light visible to human eyes. Butterflies are able to see ultraviolet light, **9**

wing veins—hollow veins on a butterfly's wings. After the butterfly expands its wings by pumping fluid though these veins, they dry and harden, **8**